D1528322

Monkeys

FIRST EDITION
Series Editor Deborah Lock; **US Editor** Shannon Beatty; **Designer** Vikas Sachdeva;
Project Designer Akanksha Gupta; **Art Director** Martin Wilson; **Production Editor** Sarah Isle;
Jacket Designer Natalie Godwin; **Reading Consultant** Linda Gambrell, PhD

THIS EDITION
Editorial Management by Oriel Square
Produced for DK by WonderLab Group LLC
Jennifer Emmett, Erica Green, Kate Hale, *Founders*

Editors Grace Hill Smith, Libby Romero, Michaela Weglinski;
Photography Editors Kelley Miller, Annette Kiesow, Nicole DiMella;
Managing Editor Rachel Houghton; **Designers** Project Design Company; **Researcher** Michelle Harris;
Copy Editor Lori Merritt; **Indexer** Connie Binder; **Proofreader** Larry Shea;
Reading Specialist Dr. Jennifer Albro; **Curriculum Specialist** Elaine Larson

Published in the United States by DK Publishing
1745 Broadway, 20th Floor, New York, NY 10019
Copyright © 2023 Dorling Kindersley Limited
DK, a Division of Penguin Random House LLC
23 24 25 26 10 9 8 7 6 5 4 3 2 1
001-333983-June/2023

A catalog record for this book
is available from the Library of Congress.
HC ISBN: 978-0-7440-7312-6
PB ISBN: 978-0-7440-7313-3

DK books are available at special discounts when purchased in bulk for sales promotions, premiums,
fundraising, or educational use. For details, contact: DK Publishing Special Markets,
1745 Broadway, 20th Floor, New York, NY 10019
SpecialSales@dk.com

Printed and bound in China

The publisher would like to thank the following for their kind permission to reproduce their images:
a=above; c=center; b=below; l=left; r=right; t=top; b/g=background

Alamy Stock Photo: WILDLIFE GmbH 9clb; **Dreamstime.com:** GCapture 12cr, Grayfoxx1942 29br,
Francisco Javier Zea Lara 29t, Sergey Uryadnikov 20cb, Wirestock 28bl, Vladyslav Zakharevych 12cl;
Getty Images: Design Pics / Brian Guzzetti 9cra, DigitalVision / Life On White 7br, Moment /
Matthias Haker Photography 7cra, Photodisc / Brand X Pictures 4-5; **Minden Pictures:** Mitsuyoshi Tatematsu 8bl;
Shutterstock.com: Jolanda Aalbers 6cl, Filipe.Lopes 6tr, MirasWonderland 7tl, Neelsky 6tl

Cover images: *Front:* **Shutterstock.com:** AnnstasAg b/g, tratong c;
Back: **Dreamstime.com:** Showvector clb; Ylivdesign cla, cra; *Spine:* **Shutterstock.com:** tratong

All other images © Dorling Kindersley
For more information see: www.dkimages.com

For the curious
www.dk.com

Monkeys

DK

Contents

Hello, Monkeys!

Meet the
monkeys of
the world.

Pygmy Marmosets

A pygmy marmoset can fit in your hand. It's the smallest monkey in the world!

claw

tail

golden fur

Tamarins

Golden lion tamarins climb up tree trunks. They run along branches.

hands

Capuchins

Capuchin monkeys eat fruit and insects, and even crabs and eggs.

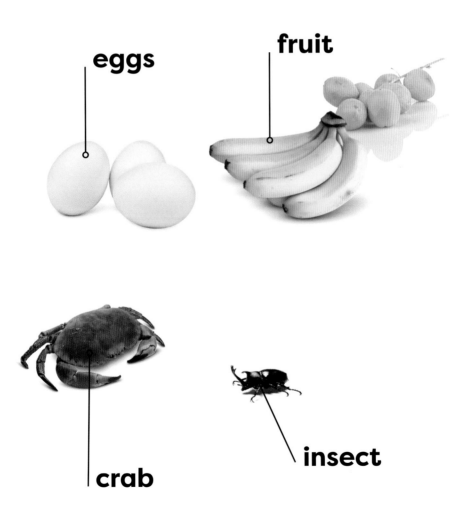

eggs

fruit

crab

insect

Squirrel Monkeys

A squirrel monkey jumps from tree to tree. Its baby hangs on.

baby

hand

Howler Monkeys

Howler monkeys call to each other. They are the loudest land animals.

ear

mouth

17

Proboscis Monkeys

Proboscis monkeys have huge noses and big bellies.

nose

belly

Macaques

Japanese macaques keep warm in the hot springs on cold days.

snow

hot spring

Mandrills

A mandrill
shows its teeth
to make friends
or scare foes.

nose

teeth

Vervet Monkeys

Vervet monkeys help each other to keep clean.

fur

foot

Baboons

A troop of baboons
live together.

Goodnight, Monkeys!

The monkeys rest
after a busy day.

Shh!

Glossary

Claw
a sharp nail on
the end of an animal's
hands or toes

Fur
a thick coat of soft
hair that covers an
animal's skin

Tail
a long, movable
body part joined to
an animal's bottom

Teeth
these are used
for biting and
chewing food

Troop
a group of monkeys,
also called a tribe

Index

Quiz

Answer the questions to see what you have learned. Check your answers with an adult.

1. Which monkey is small enough to fit on your hand?

2. What features does a proboscis monkey have?

3. Which monkey has a brightly colored nose and sharp teeth?

4. What is a group of baboons called?

5. Tell a story about your favorite monkey. What does it look like? What is it doing?

1. The pygmy marmoset 2. A huge nose and a big belly
3. A mandrill 4. A troop 5. Answers will vary